THE RANDY NEWMAN
GUITAR SONGBOOK

GUITAR TAB EDITION

MW01285171

Edited by Jim Moran

Special thanks to Jim Moran and Cathy Kerr for their assistance throughout this project

Very special thanks to Randy Newman for his invaluable input

Arrangements and transcriptions by Hemme Luttjeboer, with Jim Moran and Randy Newman

Cover photo courtesy of Pamela Springsteen

ISBN 0-7579-3718-7 (Book)

FOREWORD

I am very grateful to Hemme Luttjeboer for transcribing these songs for guitar so creatively and yet so faithfully to my original intent. The guitar is a difficult instrument to write for. I've been doing it badly for years. It's easy to write a chord sheet, G^7–C–Cm, and then pass it out to the guitar players, but on some occasions I've been compelled to put down some notes. I remember one score I did, "Michael" I think, where I wrote a lot for guitar, mandolin, etc. What I wrote looked liked the woodwind parts for the *Nutcracker Suite*—everything above the staff and moving fast. The band played it (some of the best players in the world are in Los Angeles) but I think you can hear them muttering on the soundtrack. I've gotten better but it's still a mysterious process to me.

I have nothing but the deepest respect for those of you who play the instrument. I took a guitar class once at UCLA to fulfill a performance requirement. I never got past the F chord which put two permanent grooves in the index finger of my left hand.

I hope you enjoy this. I'm glad it exists—and that it does exist has much to do with the persistence and talent of my good friend Jim Moran.

Why does Eric Clapton play only one note at a time?

Have fun.

—Randy Newman

CONTENTS

PAGE

BALTIMORE

Words and Music by
RANDY NEWMAN

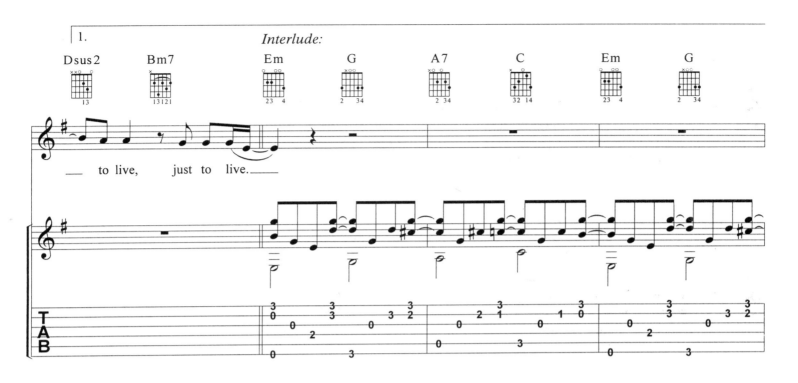

to live,   just to   live.

to live,   just to   live.

Piano *(arr. for gtr.)*

Elec. Gtr. 1

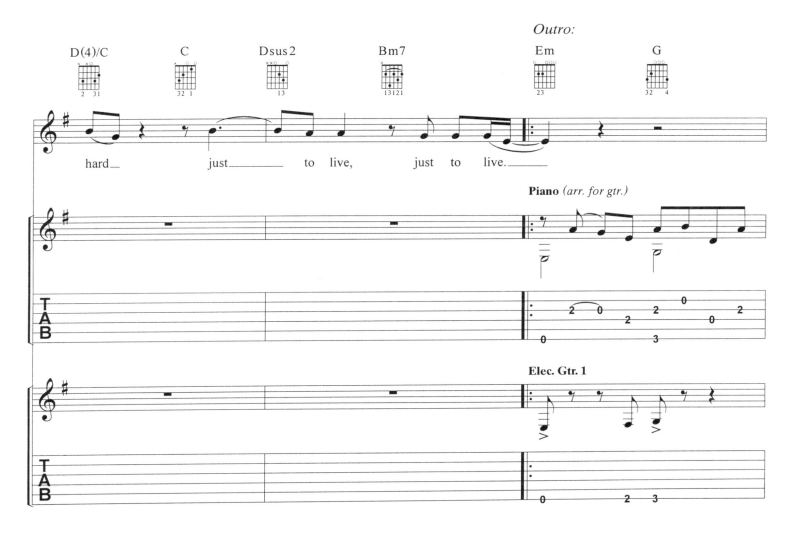

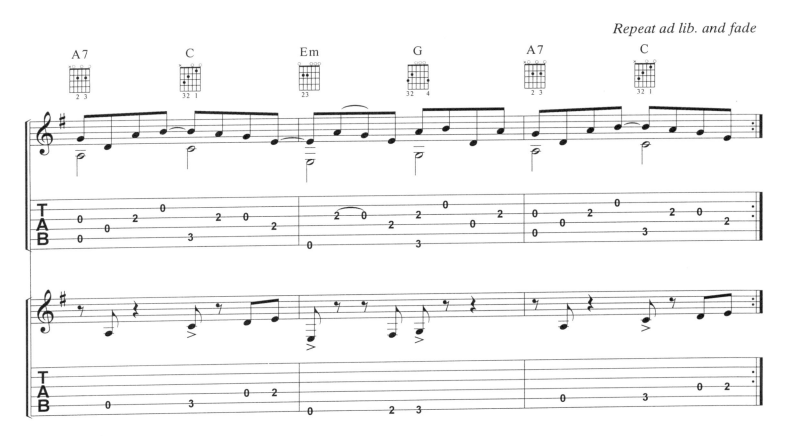

BIRMINGHAM

Words and Music by
RANDY NEWMAN

Chords for Acous. Gtr. 2 (Capo II)

Moderate swing ♩ = 104 (♫ = ♪³♪)

Intro:

Piano *(arr. for gtr.)*

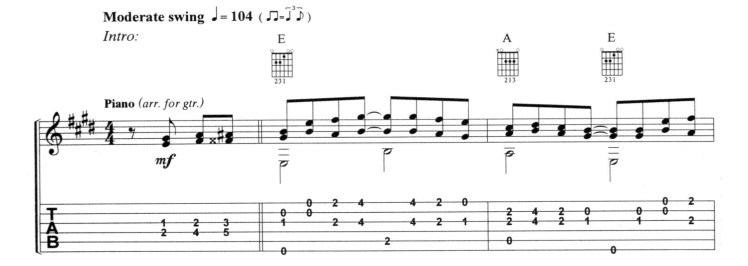

Verses 1 & 2:

Piano & Acous. Gtr. 1

1. Got a wife, got a fam -
2. My dad - dy was a bar -

12

no place like Bir - ming - ham.

Cont. in notation

Piano

To Coda

Birmingham - 5 - 3
PGM0420

Country feel

*Capoed gtr. harmony. Use frames from under the title.

Verse 3:

My wife's named__ Mar - y but she's called Ma - rie.__

We live in a___ three room house with a pep - per tree. I

work all day___ in the fac - to - ry and that's al -

Verse 4:

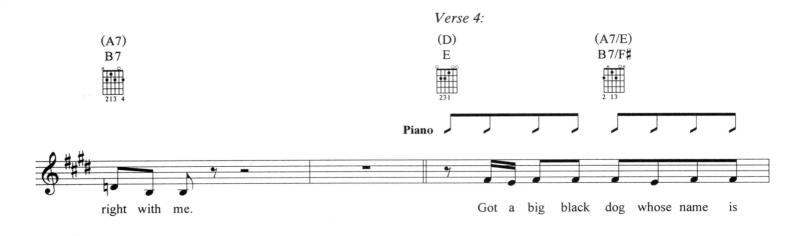

right with me. Got a big black dog whose name is

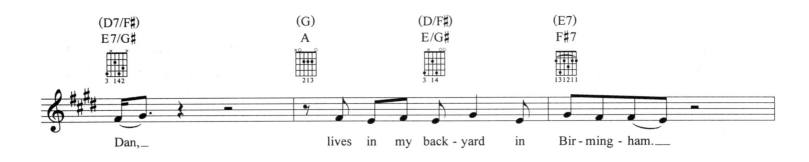

Dan,___ lives in my back-yard in Bir-ming-ham.___

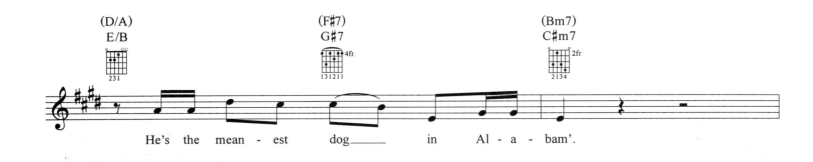

He's the mean-est dog___ in Al-a-bam'.

D.S. % al Coda Ϙ *Coda*

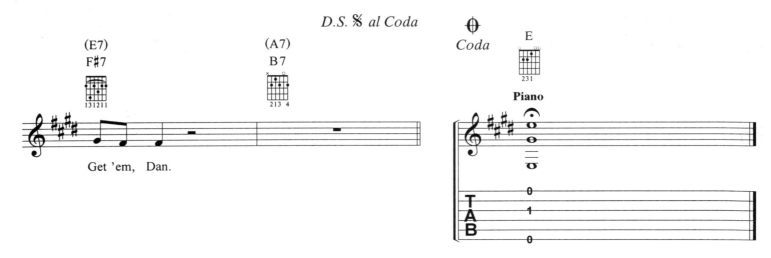

Get 'em, Dan.

GUILTY

*Gtr. capo II

Words and Music by
RANDY NEWMAN

Moderately slow blues ♩. = 60

Intro:

Verse:

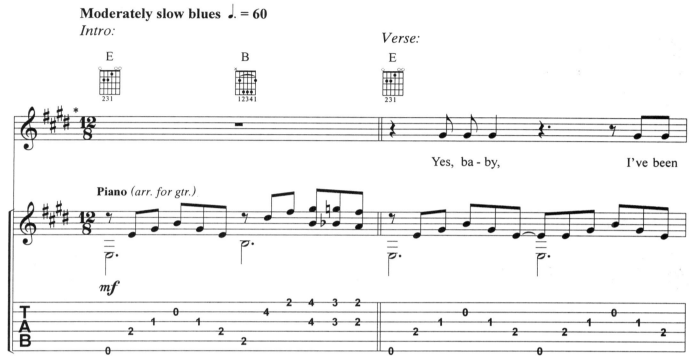

*To match record key, capo at 2nd fret.

Yes, ba - by, I've been

Piano (arr. for gtr.)

mf

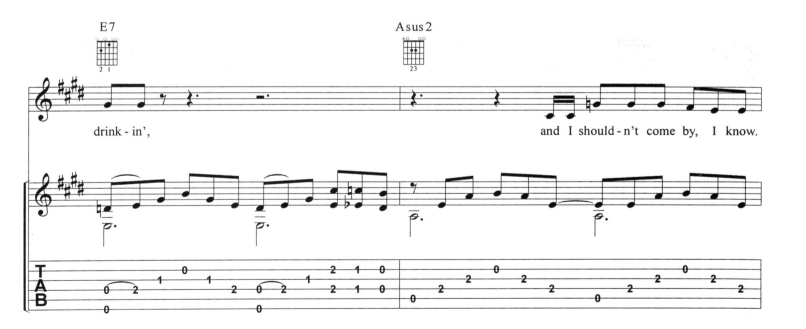

drink - in', and I should - n't come by, I know.

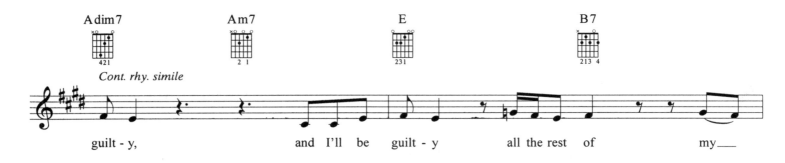

guilt - y,   and I'll be guilt - y   all the rest of   my____

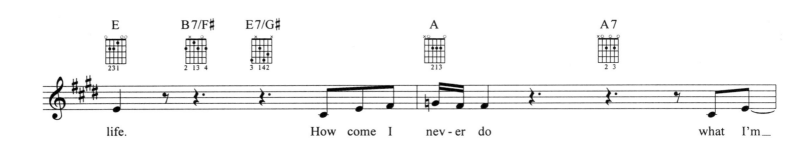

life.   How come I nev - er do   what I'm____

____ sup - posed to do?   How come noth - in' that I try to do   ev - er turns out

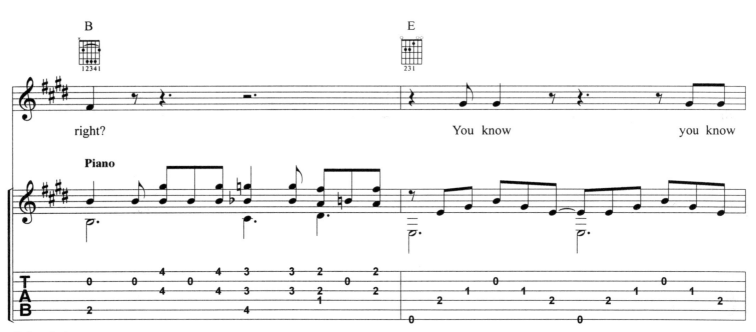

right?   You know   you know

Piano

BURN ON
(Big River)

*Gtr. capo II

Moderately ♩ = 120

Intro:

Words and Music by
RANDY NEWMAN

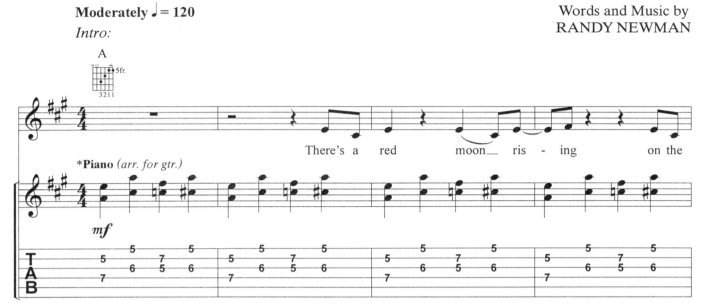

There's a red moon ris - ing on the

Piano (arr. for gtr.)

mf

*To match record key, capo at 2nd fret.

Cuy - a - ho - ga Riv - er, roll - ing in - to Cleve - land to the lake.

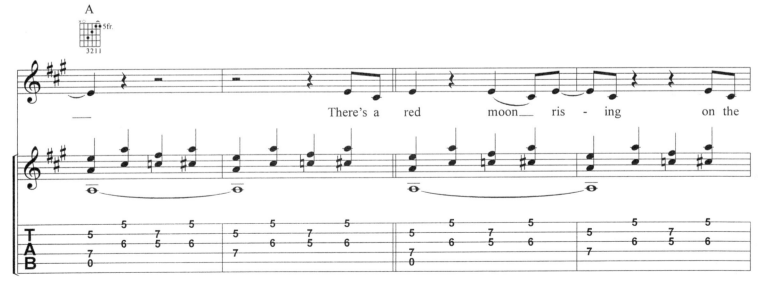

There's a red moon ris - ing on the

Burn On - 6 - 1
PGM0420

Outro Chorus:

FEELS LIKE HOME

Words and Music by
RANDY NEWMAN

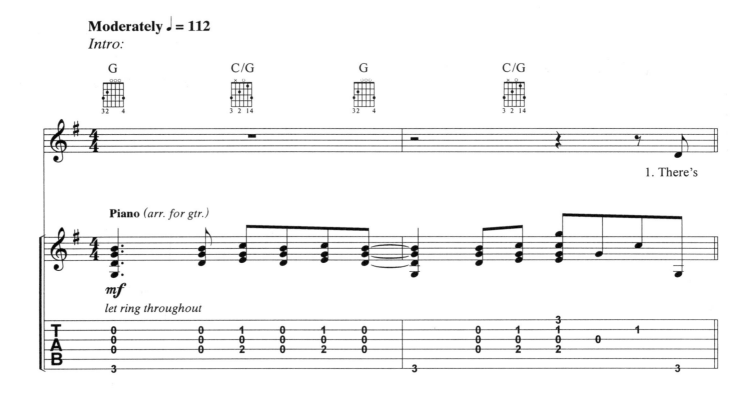

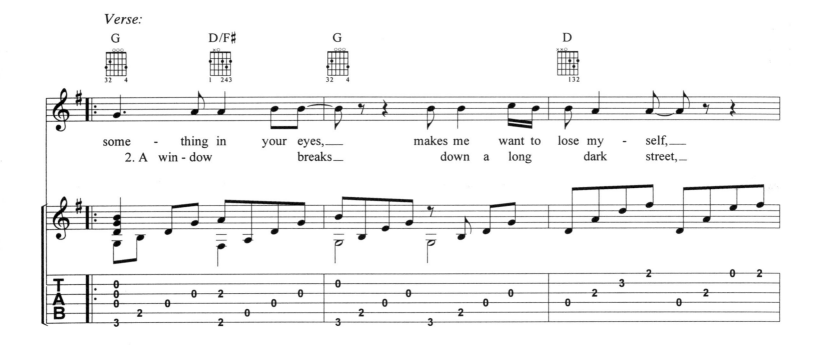

I LOVE L.A.

Words and Music by
RANDY NEWMAN

I Love L.A. - 9 - 4

PGM0420

38

I Love L.A. - 9 - 7
PGM0420

40

I LOVE TO SEE YOU SMILE

Words and Music by
RANDY NEWMAN

Moderate ragtime feel ♩ = 108

Intro:

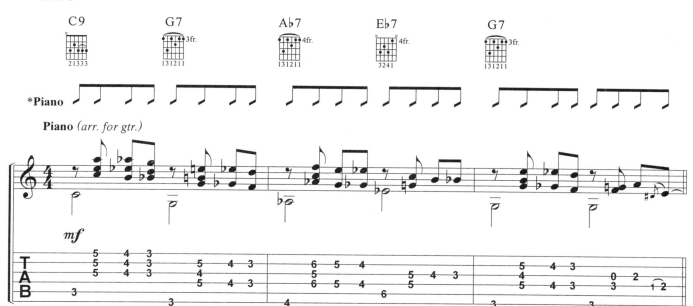

*Play this rhythmic figure throughout as an alternate pick-style version.

Verse:

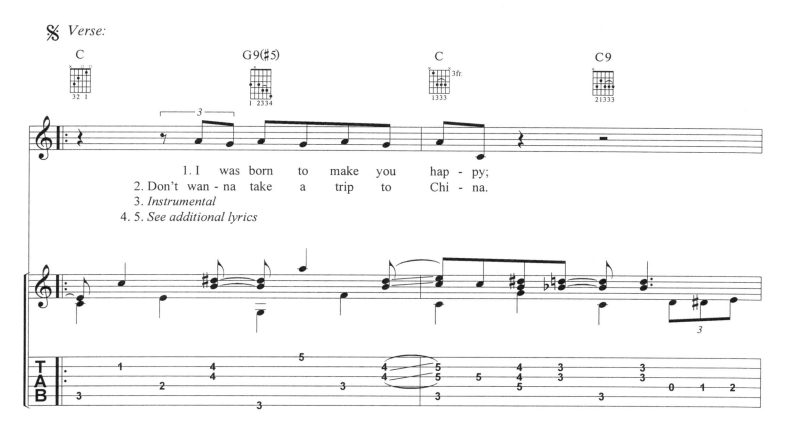

1. I was born to make you hap-py;
2. Don't wan-na take a trip to Chi-na.
3. *Instrumental*
4. 5. *See additional lyrics*

I Love to See You Smile - 5 - 1
PGM0420

42

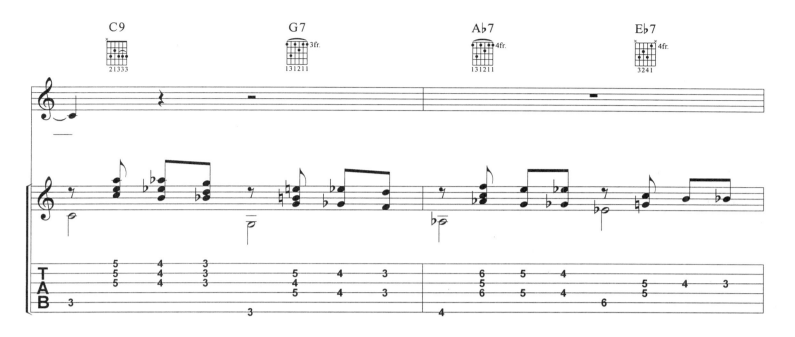

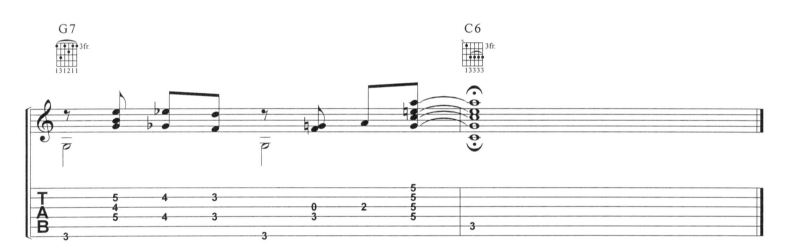

Verse 3:
(Instrumental)

Verse 4:
Like a sink without a faucet,
Like a watch without a dial,
What would I do if I didn't have you?
I love to see you smile.

Verse 5:
In a world that's full of trouble,
You make it all worthwhile.
What would I do if I didn't have you?
I just love to see you smile.
I love to see you smile.

I MISS YOU

Words and Music by
RANDY NEWMAN

I Miss You - 6 - 2
PGM0420

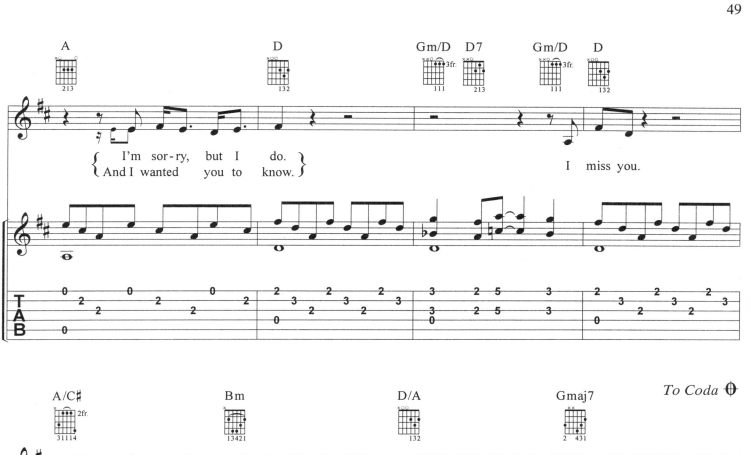

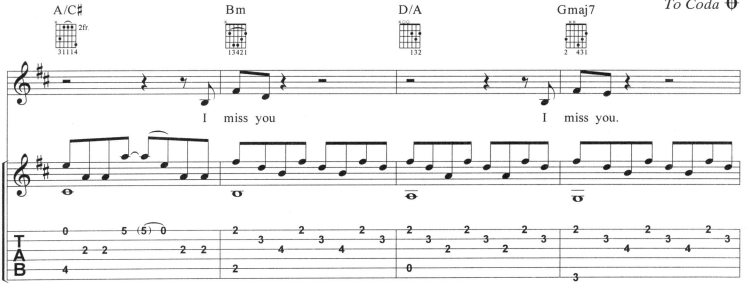

D.S. % al Coda

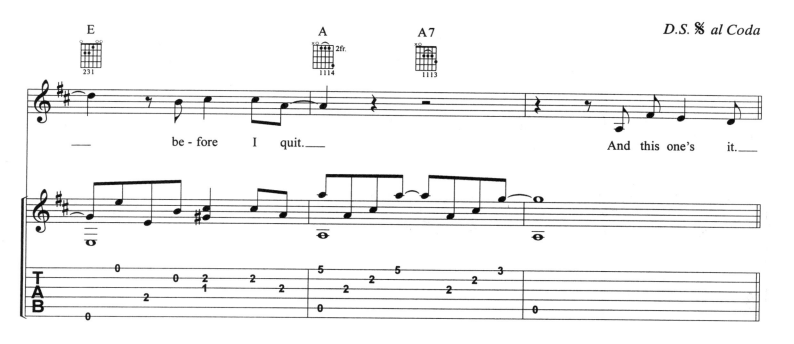

be - fore   I   quit.___   And   this one's   it.___

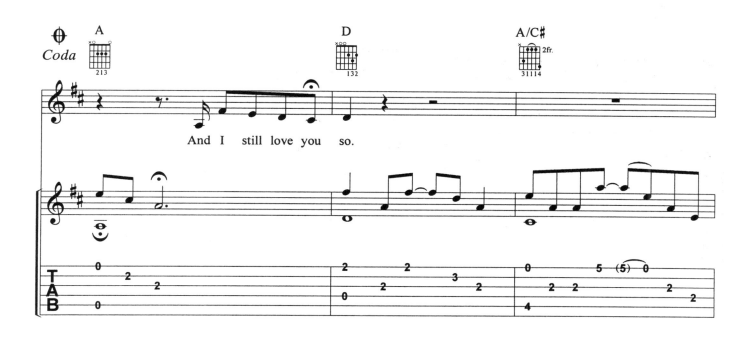

And   I   still love you   so.

I THINK IT'S GOING TO RAIN TODAY

Words and Music by
RANDY NEWMAN

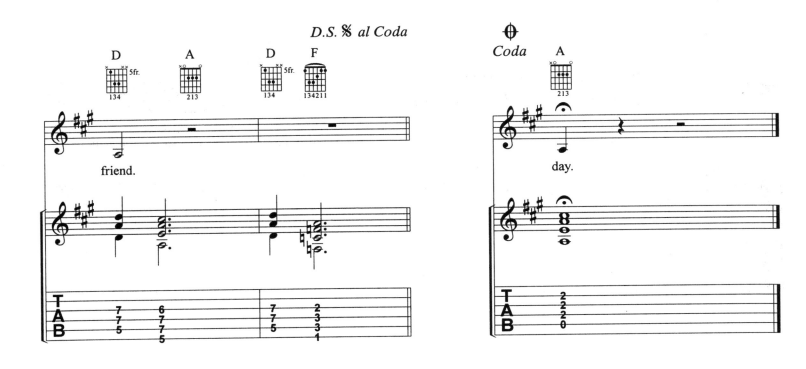

Verse 3:
Bright before me,
The signs implore me,
"Help the needy
And show them the way."
Human kindness is overflowing
And I think it's going to rain today.

LIVING WITHOUT YOU

Moderately slow ♩ = 56

Intro:

Words and Music by
RANDY NEWMAN

Piano *(arr. for gtr.)*

1. The

Verse:

mile truck hauls___ the sun up,___ the pa-per hits the
2. Ev-'ry-one's___ got some-thing.___ They're out try'n' to get___ some more.

door. The sub-way shakes my___ floor and I think a-bout___
They got some-thing to___ get up___ for. But I ain't a-bout___

Living Without You - 3 - 1
PGM0420

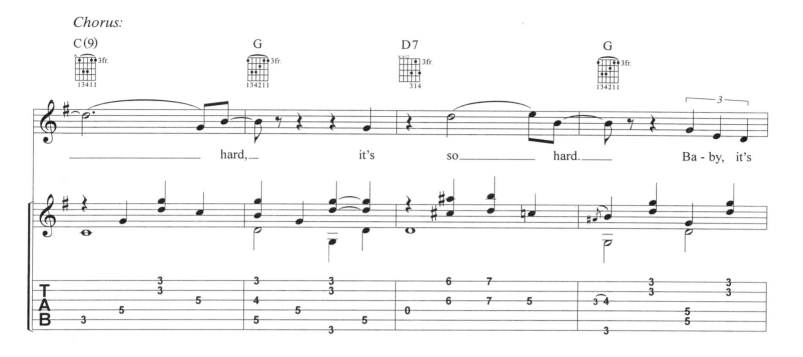

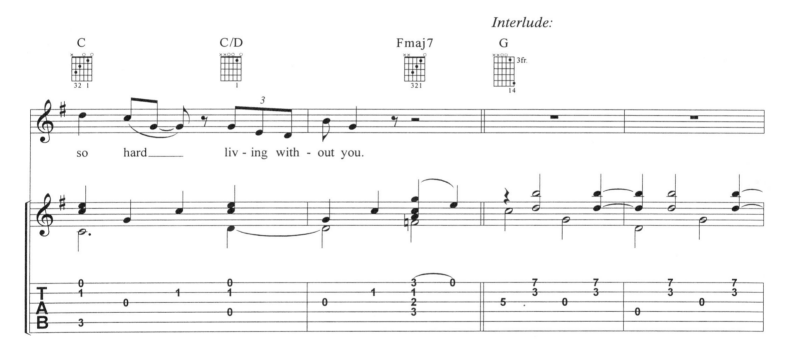

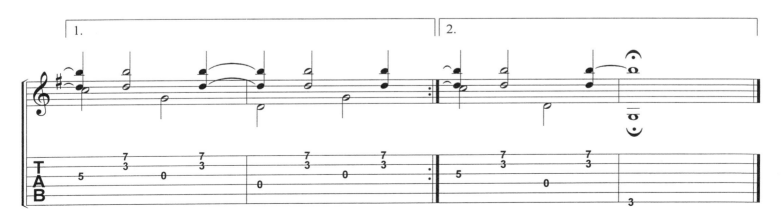

IT'S LONELY AT THE TOP

Words and Music by
RANDY NEWMAN

It's Lonely at the Top - 5 - 1
PGM0420

It's Lonely at the Top - 5 - 2
PGM0420

It's Lonely at the Top - 5 - 3
PGM0420

It's Lonely at the Top - 5 - 4
PGM0420

MAMA TOLD ME NOT TO COME

Words and Music by
RANDY NEWMAN

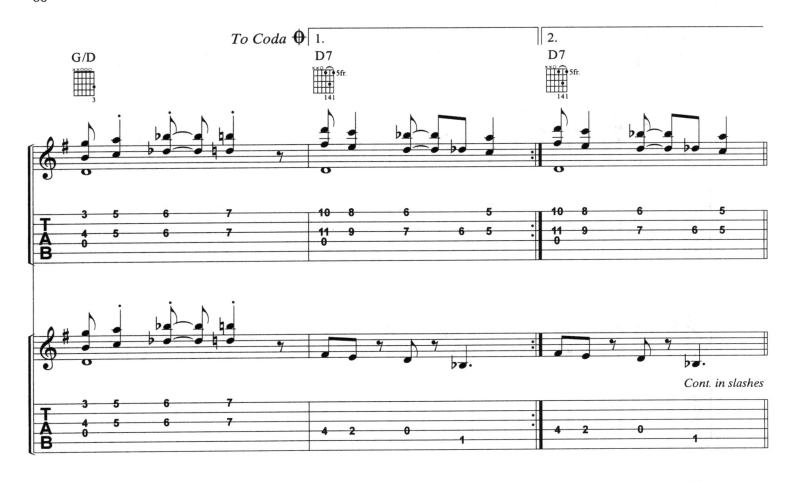

Outro:

Repeat and fade

Verse 3:
The radio is blasting,
Someone's beating on the door.
Our hostess is not lasting,
She's out on the floor.
I've seen so many things that I ain't
Never see before.
I don't know what it is,
But I don't wanna see no more.
(To Chorus:)

LOUISIANA 1927

Words and Music by
RANDY NEWMAN

70

Verse 3:
President Coolidge come down in railroad train
With a little fat man with a note-pad in his hand.
President say, "Little fat man, isn't it a shame
What the river has done to this poor cracker's land?"
(To Chorus:)

MARIE

Words and Music by
RANDY NEWMAN

Marie - 4 - 2
PGM0420

74

Marie - 4 - 3
PGM0420

75

Marie - 4 - 4
PGM0420

POLITICAL SCIENCE

Words and Music by
RANDY NEWMAN

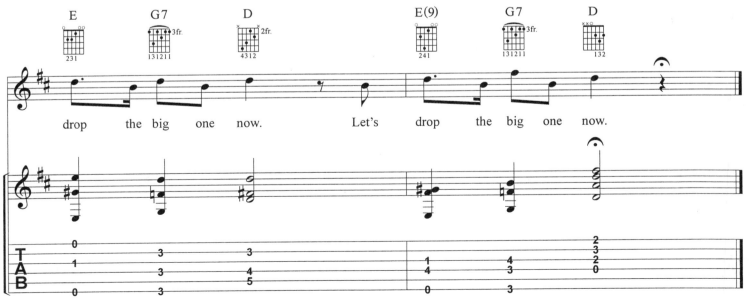

REDNECKS

Words and Music by
RANDY NEWMAN

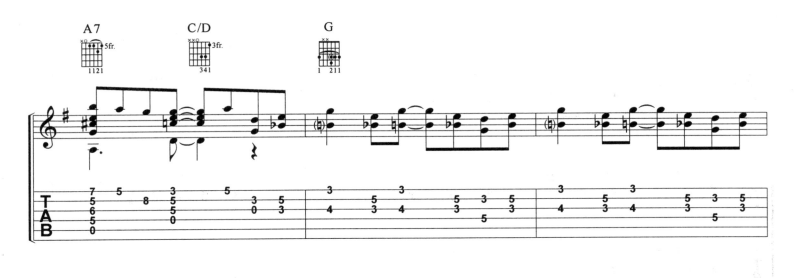

Verse 3:

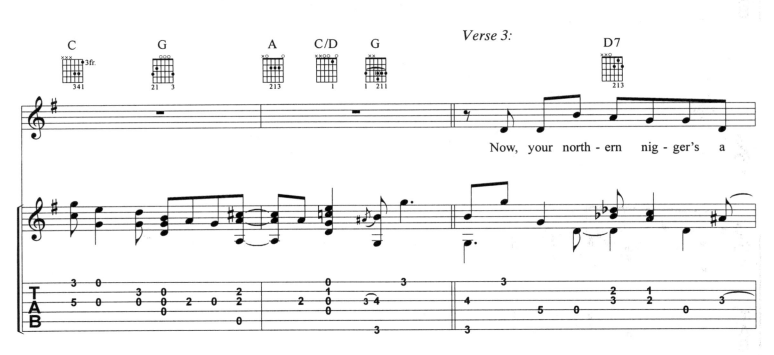

Now, your north - ern nig - ger's a

Ne - gro.   You see, he's got his dig - ni - ty.

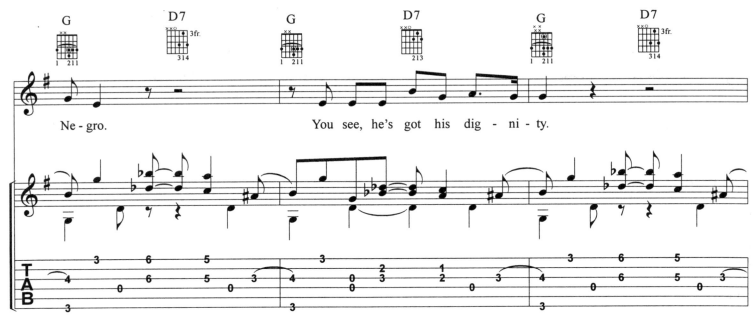

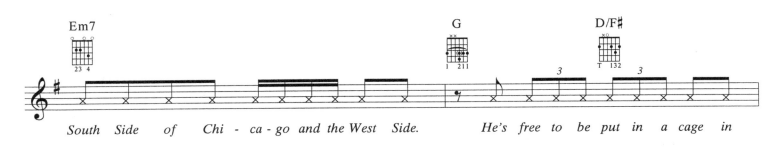

South Side of Chi - ca - go and the West Side. *He's free to be put in a cage in*

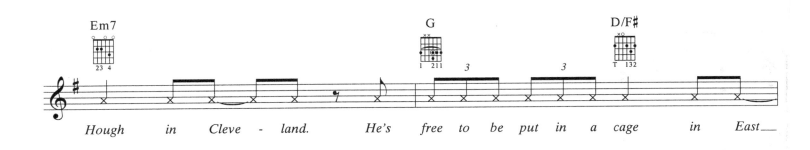

Hough in Cleve - land. He's free to be put in a cage in East____

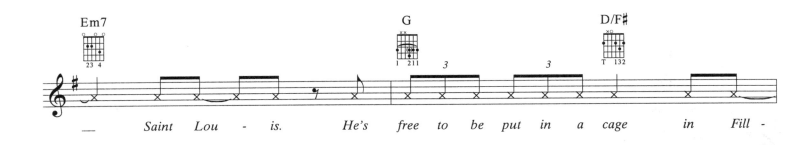

____ Saint Lou - is. He's free to be put in a cage in Fill -

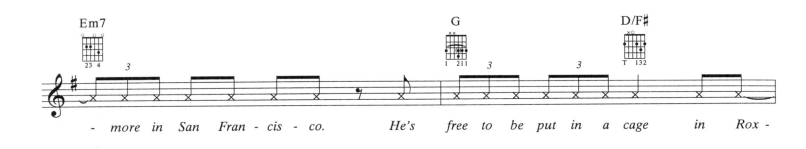

- more in San Fran - cis - co. He's free to be put in a cage in Rox -

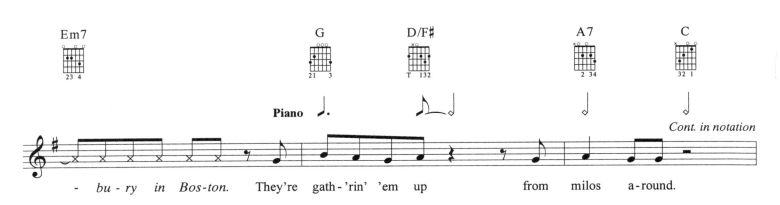

- bu - ry in Bos - ton. They're gath - 'rin' 'em up from milos a - round.

SAIL AWAY

Words and Music by
RANDY NEWMAN

SHORT PEOPLE

Words and Music by
RANDY NEWMAN

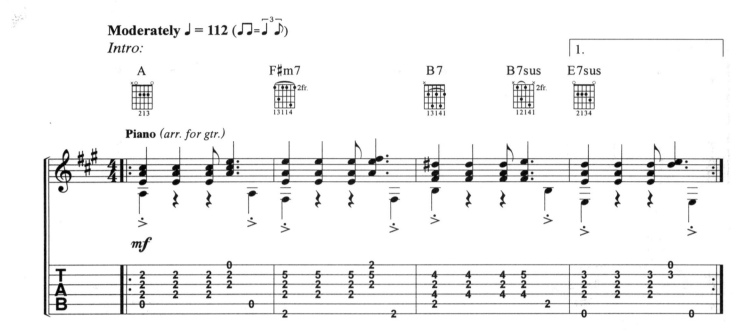

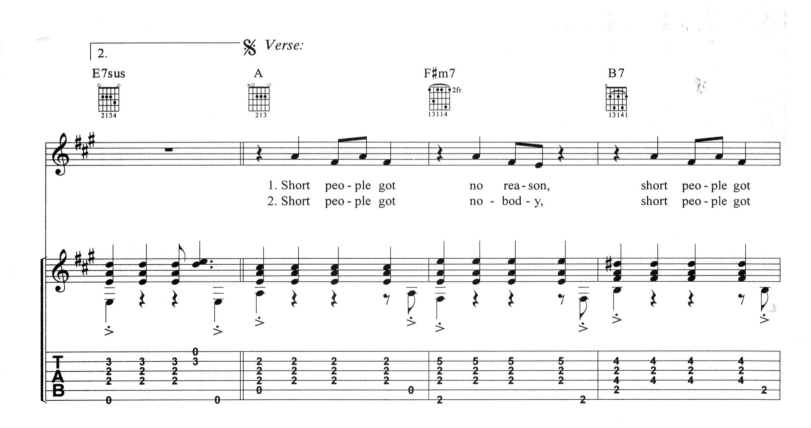

Short People - 6 - 2
PGM0420

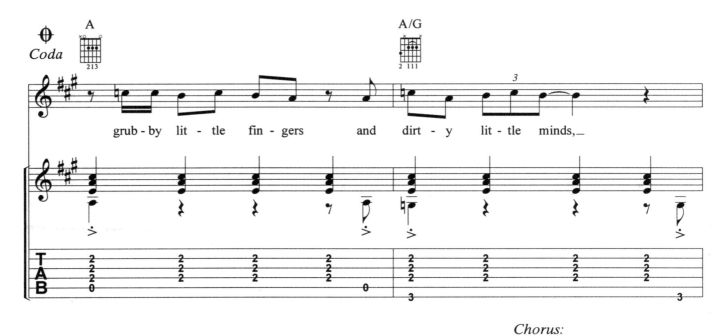

Coda

grub - by lit - tle fin - gers and dirt - y lit - tle minds,_

Chorus:

they're gon - na get you ev - 'ry time._ Well, I don't want no

*Elec. gtr. w/partial distortion doubles downstemmed notes.

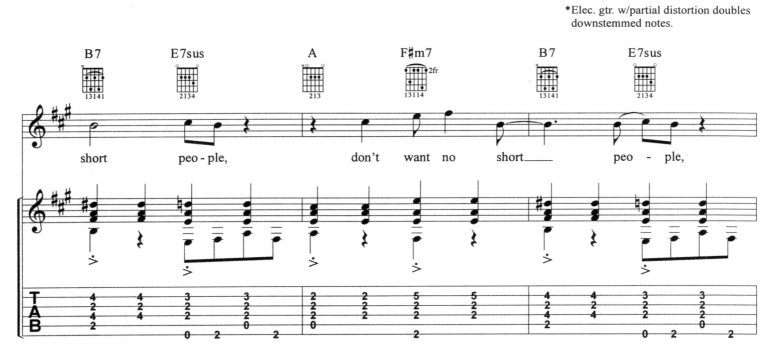

short peo - ple, don't want no short___ peo - ple,

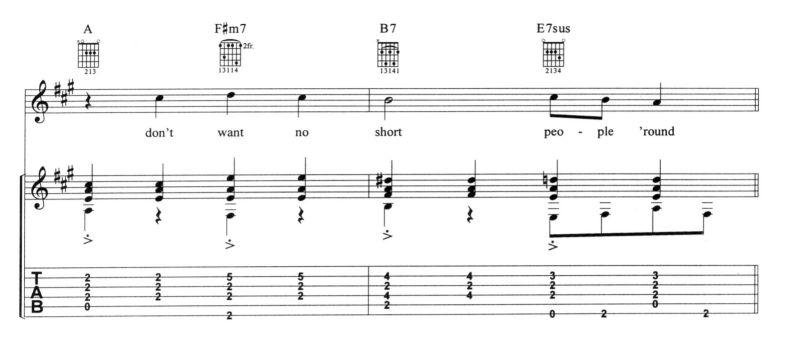

Outro:

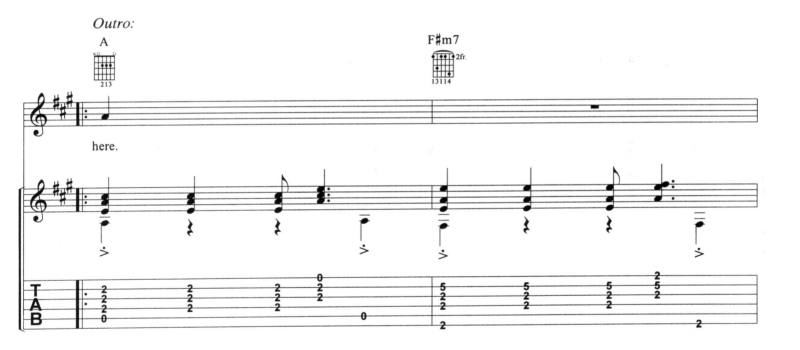

Repeat ad lib. and fade

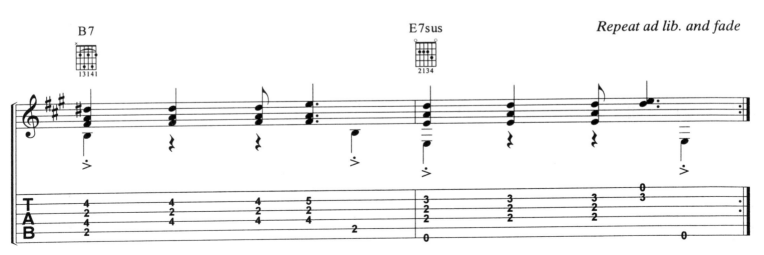

YOU CAN LEAVE YOUR HAT ON

Words and Music by
RANDY NEWMAN

*Refer to last page for an optional fingerstyle version of the introductory piano part.

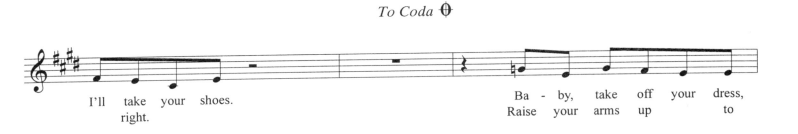

You Can Leave Your Hat On - 5 - 2

PGM0420

leave you hat on.
You give me a rea-son to live.
You can leave your hat on.
You give me a rea-son to live. You give me a rea-son to live.

You can leave_ your hat on.
You give me a rea-son to live._

Interlude:

D.S. ℅ al Coda

You Can Leave Your Hat On - 5 - 3
PGM0420

Verse 3:
Suspicious minds are talking,
Try'n' to tear us apart.
They say that my love is wrong,
They don't know what love is.
They don't know what love is.
They don't know what love is.
They don't know what love is.
I know what love is.

Optional fingerstyle arrangement of the introductory piano riff:

YOU'VE GOT A FRIEND IN ME

*Gtr. capo III

Words and Music by
RANDY NEWMAN

*To match record key, capo at 3rd fret.

You've Got a Friend in Me - 5 - 1

PGM0420

109

You're gon - na see it's our des - ti - ny.

Cont. in slashes

Chorus:

Piano *Cont. rhy. simile*

You've got a friend in me.___ You've got a friend in me.___

Yeah, you've___ got a friend in me.

Outro:

Piano

Woodwinds

You've Got a Friend in Me - 5 - 5
PGM0420

GUITAR TAB GLOSSARY **

TABLATURE EXPLANATION

READING TABLATURE: Tablature illustrates the six strings of the guitar. Notes and chords are indicated by the placement of fret numbers on a given string(s).

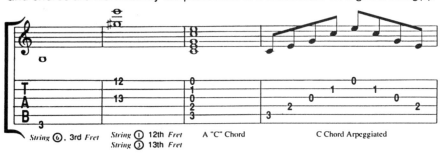

String ⑥, 3rd Fret   String ① 12th Fret   A "C" Chord   C Chord Arpeggiated
                 String ③ 13th Fret

BENDING NOTES

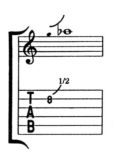

HALF STEP: Play the note and bend string one half step.*

WHOLE STEP: Play the note and bend string one whole step.

WHOLE STEP AND A HALF: Play the note and bend string a whole step and a half.

TWO STEPS: Play the note and bend string two whole steps.

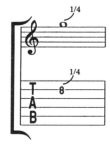

SLIGHT BEND (Microtone): Play the note and bend string slightly to the equivalent of half a fret.

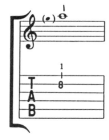

PREBEND (Ghost Bend): Bend to the specified note, before the string is picked.

PREBEND AND RELEASE: Bend the string, play it, then release to the original note.

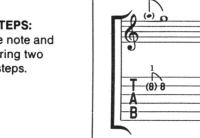

REVERSE BEND: Play the already-bent string, then immediately drop it down to the fretted note.

BEND AND RELEASE: Play the note and gradually bend to the next pitch, then release to the original note. Only the first note is attacked.

BENDS INVOLVING MORE THAN ONE STRING: Play the note and bend string while playing an additional note (or notes) on another string(s). Upon release, relieve pressure from additional note(s), causing original note to sound alone.

BENDS INVOLVING STATIONARY NOTES: Play notes and bend lower pitch, then hold until release begins (indicated at the point where line becomes solid).

UNISON BEND: Play both notes and immediately bend the lower note to the same pitch as the higher note.

DOUBLE NOTE BEND: Play both notes and immediately bend both strings simultaneously.

*A half step is the smallest interval in Western music; it is equal to one fret. A whole step equals two frets.

© 1990 Beam Me Up Music
c/o CPP/Belwin, Inc. Miami, Florida 33014
International Copyright Secured   Made in U.S.A.   All Rights Reserved   **By Kenn Chipkin and Aaron Stang

RHYTHM SLASHES

STRUM INDICATIONS: Strum with indicated rhythm.

The chord voicings are found on the first page of the transcription underneath the song title.

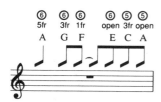

INDICATING SINGLE NOTES USING RHYTHM SLASHES: Very often single notes are incorporated into a rhythm part. The note name is indicated above the rhythm slash with a fret number and a string indication.

ARTICULATIONS

HAMMER ON: Play lower note, then "hammer on" to higher note with another finger. Only the first note is attacked.

LEFT HAND HAMMER: Hammer on the first note played on each string with the left hand.

PULL OFF: Play higher note, then "pull off" to lower note with another finger. Only the first note is attacked.

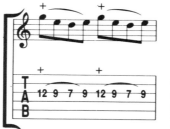

FRET-BOARD TAPPING: "Tap" onto the note indicated by + with a finger of the pick hand, then pull off to the following note held by the fret hand.

TAP SLIDE: Same as fretboard tapping, but the tapped note is slid randomly up the fretboard, then pulled off to the following note.

BEND AND TAP TECHNIQUE: Play note and bend to specified interval. While holding bend, tap onto note indicated.

LEGATO SLIDE: Play note and slide to the following note. (Only first note is attacked).

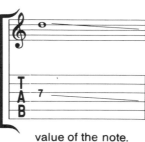

LONG GLISSAN-DO: Play note and slide in specified direction for the full value of the note.

SHORT GLISSAN-DO: Play note for its full value and slide in specified direction at the last possible moment.

PICK SLIDE: Slide the edge of the pick in specified direction across the length of the string(s).

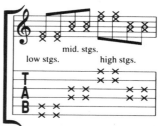

MUTED STRINGS: A percussive sound is made by laying the fret hand across all six strings while pick hand strikes specified area (low, mid, high strings).

PALM MUTE: The note or notes are muted by the palm of the pick hand by lightly touching the string(s) near the bridge.

TREMOLO PICKING: The note or notes are picked as fast as possible.

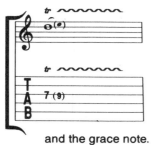

TRILL: Hammer on and pull off consecutively and as fast as possible between the original note and the grace note.

ACCENT: Notes or chords are to be played with added emphasis.

STACCATO (Detached Notes): Notes or chords are to be played roughly half their actual value and with separation.

DOWN STROKES AND UPSTROKES: Notes or chords are to be played with either a downstroke (⊓ .) or upstroke (∨) of the pick.

VIBRATO: The pitch of a note is varied by a rapid shaking of the fret hand finger, wrist, and forearm.

HARMONICS

NATURAL HARMONIC: A finger of the fret hand lightly touches the note or notes indicated in the tab and is played by the pick hand.

ARTIFICIAL HARMONIC: The first tab number is fretted, then the pick hand produces the harmonic by using a finger to lightly touch the same string at the second tab number (in parenthesis) and is then picked by another finger.

ARTIFICIAL "PINCH" HAR-MONIC: A note is fretted as indicated by the tab, then the pick hand produces the harmonic by squeezing the pick firmly while using the tip of the index finger in the pick attack. If parenthesis are found around the fretted note, it does not sound. No parenthesis means both the fretted note and A.H. are heard simultaneously.

TREMOLO BAR

SPECIFIED INTERVAL: The pitch of a note or chord is lowered to a specified interval and then may or may not return to the original pitch. The activity of the tremolo bar is graphically represented by peaks and valleys.

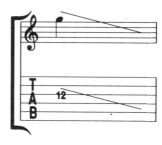

UN-SPECIFIED INTERVAL: The pitch of a note or a chord is lowered to an unspecified interval.